TO...

FROM..

MR. MEN LITTLE MISS

Roger Hargreaves

LOVE

I'm so happy when we're together.

You bring sunshine into my life.

All my worries disappear
when I'm with you.

I know you'll be there for me through the ups and downs.

And help me bounce back
from the bumps along the way.

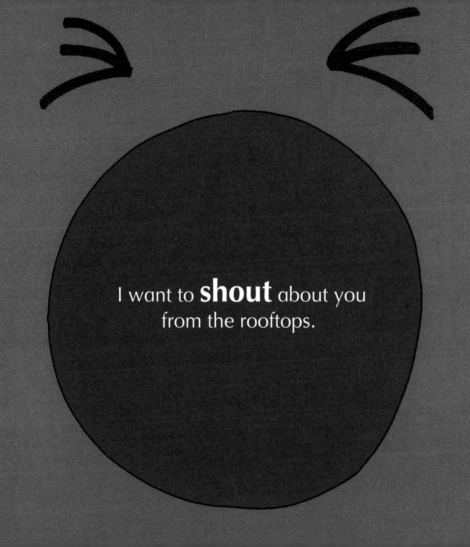

I want to **shout** about you
from the rooftops.

To broadcast to everyone
how amazing you are.

You make
me laugh a
little louder,

And live a lot more.

You make me happy whatever the weather.

You are as splendid as
Little Miss Splendid.

And as cool as Mr Cool.

And to jump for joy.

We're never stuck for words when we're together.

There's no need to be shy
with you by my side.

Life is magic with you around.

You make the impossible possible.

And the courage
to be brave.

I know you'll always
come to my rescue.

And be there with a perfectly-fitting
hug when I need it.

But I'll just say that you are
practically perfect in every way!

MR. MEN   LITTLE MISS

MR. MEN™ LITTLE MISS™ © THOIP (a Sanrio company)

First published as Mr. Men Love © 2019 THOIP (a SANRIO company)
This edition © 2023 THOIP (a SANRIO company)
Printed and published under license from Penguin Random House LLC
Published in Great Britain by Farshore
An imprint of HarperCollins*Publishers*
1 London Bridge Street, London SE1 9GF
www.farshore.co.uk

HarperCollins*Publishers*
Macken House, 39/40 Mayor Street Upper,
Dublin 1, D01 C9W8

ISBN 978 0 0085 3387 8
Printed in Italy
001

Heart image used under licence from Shutterstock.com

Stay safe online. Farshore is not responsible for content hosted by third parties.

MIX
Paper | Supporting
responsible forestry
FSC FSC™ C007454

This book is produced from independently certified FSC™ paper
to ensure responsible forest management.

For more information visit: www.harpercollins.co.uk/green